SECRETS
OF
SUCCESSFUL
PHARMACEUTICAL
SALESPEOPLE

Secrets
of
Successful
Pharmaceutical
Salespeople

By

Sarah Taylor

Taylor Presentations
Gig Harbor, Washington

Secrets of Successful
Pharmaceutical Salespeople

Published by:
Taylor Presentations
Gig Harbor, WA 98335
www.TaylorPresentations.com
Sarah@TaylorPresentations.com

ISBN 0-9764414-0-3

Cover by Alchemy Graphics
Printed by Central Plains Book Manufacturing

**Dedicated to every rep
who strives to be the very best.**

TABLE OF CONTENTS

Acknowledgments 9

Introduction 11

Secret #1: Don't Make Eight Calls a Day 15

Secret #2: Plan Your Calls Differently 23

Secret #3: Know More Science 31

Secret #4: Get in the Door 37

Secret #5: Target Your Message 45

Secret #6: Close the Sale 55

Secret #7: Don't Get Too Close! 61

Secret #8: Be Positive 67

Secret #9: Be Ethical 75

Secret #10: Enjoy Your Job 83

Conclusion 89

About Sarah Taylor 93

What Others Are Saying 95

ACKNOWLEDGMENTS

This book could not have been written without the support, belief and hard work of many people. I would like to begin by thanking my husband, Mark Taylor, MD, who encouraged me throughout this process – even during the long procrastination phase! I am blessed to have found my soul mate. I will always be grateful to my parents, George and Virginia Kenefick, for teaching me to believe that I can do anything I set my mind to do. The confidence they instilled in me is perhaps the biggest factor in the completion of this book. I couldn't ask for better parents. My sister, Karen Kenefick is an incredible role model. She exemplifies success in so many areas of her life, but most importantly in character. I am proud to call her my sister. My best friend, Carol Schaeffer, has believed in me perhaps the most. Her friendship has helped me grow professionally, personally and spiritually, and I will always be grateful for her presence in my life.

I would also like to thank the people who either helped me directly or indirectly with this book. Some of them spent many hours assisting me, and I will always be grateful: Richard W. Bowne; Sharon Galbraith; Ja Marr Brown; Michael DeLapp; James Peace, MD; Kenneth Smith; Alissa Brodin; Jason Bacharach, MD; George A. Cioffi, MD; Terri Dunevant; Amy Welch; Danielle Brown; Tina Rodriguez; Michael Mockovak, MD and my mentors and friends at Toastmasters.

Special thanks to the people who contributed to the physical creation of this book: Matthew Finn and Joleen Stenbak at Alchemy Graphics/Sign Express, Melody Morris at Central Plains Book Manufacturing, Jim and Barb Weems at Ad Graphics and Kate Hinely, Editor. Thank you all for providing impeccable quality under tight deadlines!

Most importantly, I will always be indebted to the "Successful Pharmaceutical Salespeople" who made this book a reality. Each person interviewed for this book was asked if they would like to remain anonymous, and many of them did. Since those who chose to remain anonymous will not find satisfaction in seeing their names in print, I hope they will find satisfaction in seeing their comments in print, and in knowing that they have helped thousands of other representatives to refine their business practices and aim for success. For those who chose to accept written credit for their input, I would like to thank Susan Alexander, Tina Belcastro, Richard W. Bowne, Charlotte Cavoores, Penny Davis, André Ellison, Andrea Gibson, Tiffany Grosvenor, Gregory Higa, Stacy Johnson, Karen Kenefick, Deepak Massand, Chris McFaul, Rob Ryan, and Peter Stankovich.

I am inspired by you all and by your remarkable success!

Sarah

INTRODUCTION

Perhaps you just got your first job in the pharmaceutical industry – or maybe you've been in the industry for years. Look around. You will notice that some people get *exceptional* results year after year after year. Not an awards banquet goes by where they aren't on stage – usually for the most coveted honors.

People who get pharmaceutical sales jobs in the first place are generally very high performers. Anecdotally, they were often in the top 10% academically (and socially) in high school, and in college they were usually involved in sororities or fraternities, campus clubs and sports, and many were on the Dean's List. Pharmaceutical representatives (reps) are used to excelling and they expect to excel. Yet when they are thrown into a company comprised of other high achievers, the law of averages states that most representatives' sales results will fall into the range of "average" – that big middle area under the bell-shaped curve. When this happens, most reps have a *very* hard time believing it – it is often the first time in their life that they have not been at the top of their class. Faced with the prospect of mediocrity, many of these reps will blame outside factors such as formularies, the marketing department, company policies, whoever set their sales objective, or the state of the industry. But the fact is that the top performers are facing exactly the same challenges, and they *still* excel … year after year after year.

This book will show you the secrets of those top performers, their managers, and their executives. Find out exactly what they do on a daily basis to get where they are …

and stay there. Find out how they deal with difficult customers, low access and restrictive policies, and how they stay determined to excel. Follow each of these steps without fail and then go buy yourself a new suit for next year's awards banquet!

Before we begin, let me tell you about the "successful pharmaceutical salespeople" that were interviewed for this book. In general, they are in the top 5% of the nation for either their overall performance or for a specific product at their company. Each of them has won their company's highest award at least once (for most companies, this is the President's Club Award.) Several have been the #1 representative in the nation for a period of time with a major product. Some examples include #1 Prozac Sales in the Nation, #1 Nexium Sales in the Nation, #1 Timoptic XE Sales in the nation, #1 Floxin Sales in the Nation and #1 Ortho Tri-Cyclen Sales in the Nation. One of these successful salespeople even won 2nd place in the nation as "Pharmaceutical Representative of the Year" by *Pharmaceutical Representative* Magazine! They come from many different specialties in the industry including primary care, cardiology, ophthalmology, urology, hospital sales, OB/GYN, and others. Most still work in the industry, although a few have retired. Many have over 20 years experience, providing an excellent perspective on long-term success.

When reviewing this book, some people asked why I didn't interview doctors. I actually began this project including physician interviews, but quickly learned that the attributes that some doctors described about their "best reps" often did not coincide with the habits of success. For example, several doctors said the best reps respected their time and didn't try to detail them when they were busy. However, most of the reps I questioned said that they will *almost always* get in some kind of a message – even if it's very short – because doctors are *always* busy. If they walked away whenever a doctor was busy, they would never sell anything! In another example, one doctor said his "best" reps bring his staff food. However, since most reps bring food to the offices they work with, that's not a strong indicator of success. I began to realize that doctors may not be good at guessing which reps are successful.

One last comment. Everyone I interviewed was given the option of anonymity, and many did choose to remain anonymous. While I would love to share their names with you and boast about what a great group of representatives I interviewed, I am honoring their requests. I thank them immensely for their willingness to help. For a list of people who did not choose to remain anonymous please read the acknowledgments section. Please note that no one was asked about any company trade secrets, nor were they asked information about their companies, products or competitors. All questions focused on the habits and attitudes that make these reps so successful. I am sure you will benefit tremendously from hearing their secrets. This book is truly theirs, and not mine.

Enjoy!

Secret #1:

Don't Make Eight Calls a Day

Have you ever wondered how it is possible that some reps can leave their house at 10:00 am and really get in eight[1] calls before 2:00 pm? It's usually because they are making eight *calls*, not eight *details*. Particularly in primary care offices where it is becoming especially difficult to see doctors, it probably *will* take all day to detail eight doctors. You may try twenty offices to achieve those eight details, but if that's what it takes, that's what successful reps do. On rare days when they are fortunate enough to detail eight doctors by 2:00 pm, the best reps see it as an opportunity to gain a competitive advantage and detail four more doctors.

---

[1] Some companies require more or less than 8 calls per day. Please read this section keeping in mind the number of calls per day your company requires.

One of the biggest discrepancies between representatives in the industry is what each one considers a detail. Ask yourself, "What constitutes a detail when I am entering my calls into my computer at night?" For many reps, a detail consists of hanging out with the office staff, bringing gifts, chatting with the doctor about their golf game and family, getting a signature, dropping samples and then … leaving! They justify calling it a detail by saying they have "accomplished something" by building a relationship. Other reps will often a count signature and even a "hall sighting" as a detail! Successful reps *know* that signatures and hall sightings DON'T COUNT!

> **The true definition of a detail, in a successful representative's mind, is a conversation that will likely impact the doctor's behavior and positively move market share.**

A significant detail may only last one minute. On the other hand, completely insignificant calls can last half an hour – and products may never even be discussed!

Here is a good rule of thumb: If you honestly believe that your conversation will impact the doctor's behavior and positively move market share, then count it as a successful detail.

> **Poor reps count signatures as details; mediocre reps count "something accomplished" as a detail; successful reps count "something sold" as a detail.**

Remember, this is your career. If you want to be successful, it doesn't matter if you can justify counting it as a detail on your computer. No matter what you call it, you're only cheating yourself if you end your day with all calls and no details[2].

One way to determine if your detail will likely impact behavior and result in new prescriptions is by successfully overcoming a serious objection. Another might be hearing the doctor make a sincere comment that the information is new to him and will be very helpful in treating his patients. Getting the doctor to agree to read a study or discuss the drug with a specific colleague who uses the product would also likely result in more prescriptions. Of course, the best determinate of new prescriptions is getting the doctor's commitment to prescribe your drug, so Chapter 6 is entirely devoted to getting that commitment!

So what makes some reps walk away with a handful of signatures and call it a day? And why is it that some reps who began their careers detailing very strongly, now just make calls? There are many reasons, but one of the biggest reasons is simple laziness. One manager, who has been successfully producing winning reps for 14 years, said, "Some reps allow themselves to fall into a rut. They don't challenge themselves and they begin to atrophy. **You need to work as if your manager were in the car with you every day.**" He elaborated, "Show horses look good on show day (when their manager is riding with them) but sit in their stalls the rest of the time. More tenured reps seem to have a bigger problem with this because they think that since they've laid the groundwork and have built the rela-

---

[2] In practice, our industry uses the terms "call" and "detail" interchangeably. Just make sure you know the difference in *your* mind.

tionships, they can sit back. These representatives are often the ones who don't have a plan, who aren't focused..."

Another reason that some reps work less is frustration that there is no new data on their products, or that there are newer products on the market that are better. One top representative said that the biggest mistake that she sees average reps making is letting themselves become apathetic. They work hard during a launch phase or when a major study is published for their product, but otherwise don't detail their products very often. There can be long stretches of time between studies or new products when they are just "sample droppers." Another rep commented similarly, saying, "Our companies pay us to self-motivate – not just during a launch phase, but during *every* phase of our product's life cycle. If there is really nothing new to discuss with physicians, it is *our job* to scour our resources and *find* something new and interesting that we haven't shared with them before." She said that there have been droughts in new data when she has hunted through her product circular to find one or two little tidbits that she hasn't detailed about before. Then she can walk into an office and say, "Doctor, I have some new information to share with you about Product X."

Self-motivation is an interesting topic because many reps live miles or even states away from their manager, and there is no one watching them on a regular basis. If you're asking yourself, "How *do* I stay motivated when my product is old, there is no new data, and I've been doing this forever?" there is a great answer: get acquainted with motivational books and tapes. Authors like Zig Ziglar, Anthony Robbins, Napoleon Hill, Dale Carnegie and Brian Tracy are all experts who will inspire you to succeed. Their material can teach you a variety of ways to motivate yourself in all areas of your life. Techniques like organizing each day the night before, goal setting and visualization can have a tremendous impact on your motivation level. The trick is finding which authors speak to your style. Once you find those authors, read everything they ever wrote and look for more! Many pharmaceutical companies have lending libraries at their headquarters so that you can e-mail requests for these authors' work to be sent to you through the mail. Other companies may not have lending libraries, but instead have educational and training funds which you can use to purchase and expense educational books, tapes and CD's.

One successful representative, who often led the nation in sales before he was promoted to marketing, said that the company was paying him to work from 9 to 5. That time included the numerous hours he spent in his car. Therefore, he always had a handful of motivational CDs in his car that he popped into his CD player when he was driving between offices. Now *that's* the habit of a successful rep!

SUMMARY

Key Points:

- Don't make eight calls a day. Make eight details.

- To determine if your call is worthy of being called a detail, use this rule of thumb: If you honestly believe that your conversation will impact the doctor's behavior and positively move market share, then count it as a successful detail in your computer that night.

- Work as if your manager were in the car with you every day.

- Use motivational books and tapes to motivate yourself.

Key Quote:

"Poor representatives count a signature as a detail; mediocre reps count "something accomplished" as a detail; successful reps count "something sold" as a detail."

SUCCESS ASSESSMENT

1. On a typical day, what percentage of my time is spent making calls instead of details?_____

2. Is this number higher than I'd like it to be?

    Yes   No

3. If I am spending too much time making calls instead of details, why is this? (Have I become lazy? Do I feel my products aren't the best and am nervous about asking for the business? Do I feel there is nothing new to say about my products? Do I rush through my calls so I can get home early?)

    _____

    _____

    _____

    _____

4. What is one thing I can do on territory tomorrow to turn potentially ineffective calls into highly effective details?

    _____

    _____

    _____

    _____

SECRET #2:

PLAN YOUR CALLS DIFFERENTLY

Pre-call planning. What's new? Every company emphasizes the importance of pre-call planning. We all know how to do it and that we should do it, so why devote an entire chapter to it? Because many reps still aren't planning their calls – or are not planning them effectively – and there is a certain way that the most successful reps are doing it differently. Keep reading to learn their secrets!

One rep, who was once the #1 seller of the popular Floxin antibiotic, said that one mistake she made early in her career was calling on some of her toughest doctors without being 100% prepared. As a new rep, even if you graduated at the top of your training class, you are already at a disadvantage due to limited knowledge and experience. To call on one of your most important doctors without a very thorough plan could impair your credibility with that doctor for many years to come. She said that, in retrospect, "I should have asked my district manager who the toughest doctors in my territory were and hit them on the second round. It took a long time to overcome credibility issues with two doctors in particular."

But planning isn't only essential for new reps. *Every* representative can greatly increase his or her effectiveness with a solid plan for each and every call. One highly respected manager, who recently retired after 36 years in the business, said that planning is one key difference between exceptional reps and average reps. "The best reps have a plan for each day and a plan for each call. Average reps have an idea of what they want to do but not a solid plan. They bark out a marketing message, and then presume the physician will prescribe their product." We've all seen representatives who do this, and it could be that at times you've fallen victim to this approach as well. Perhaps you let yourself get tied up with administrative details or your personal life, and don't get around to planning your messages the night before. The next morning, when the doctor is standing in front of you, you end up throwing out a generic question such as, "So, doctor, how's Product X working for you?" This type of approach rarely invokes a meaningful discussion, and rarely sells anything either.

One of the reasons why these generic questions are so ineffective, and often actually harmful, is because they provoke the doctor to respond in kind. A popular sales author, Steve Schiffman, writes in his books that "people respond in kind," meaning that they follow your lead. An example that he uses in his book *Cold-Calling Techniques That Really Work* is the scenario where you walk into a clothing store and the sales clerk asks, "Can I help you find something?" You respond in kind by automatically saying, "No, thank you!" Even if you really are looking for something specific, the knee-jerk reaction is to say "No." This is no different with doctors and pharmaceutical reps. Here are a few common lines to avoid due to the knee-jerk responses you are likely to evoke:

"Doctor, do you have a few minutes to hear about Product X?"
("Not right now.")
"So how is Product X working for you?"
("Great!")
"Hi. Dr. Smith, I've got some samples of Product X for you!"
("Great! Where do I sign?")

You get the point. Maybe you get a positive answer, maybe a negative answer, but it will almost always be a knee-jerk, in-kind response, which you can never trust to be reliable.

Planning your calls ahead of time will help you to avoid asking questions that provoke a knee-jerk response. The best way to avoid an in-kind response is to ask an open-ended question (a question that can't be answered with a "yes" or "no" response). Instead of asking, "How is Product X working for you?" ask, "Now that you've had a month to try out the new dose of Product X, can you tell me how a few of your patients have responded to it?" That kind of question not only makes them think and give you a thoughtful answer, but you are likely to confirm their positive opinion of the drug or uncover an objection to them using it in the future. Whenever you successfully uncover an objection that the physician has not discussed with you before, pat yourself on the back – uncovering and overcoming objections is the only way to sell your product!

Another rep pointed out an ancillary benefit of pre-call planning: "I used to wing it a little bit. I knew my products and the doctor's prescribing habits well enough to get something satisfactory out of my mouth, but never anything extraordinary. However, during those times when I unexpectedly ended up face-to-face with a doctor who doesn't see reps or who likes to antagonize reps, I would usually get nervous and flub it up. When I got serious about planning my calls the night before, that nervousness disappeared because I knew I had a clear purpose and a message that could benefit that doctor's patients." She discovered, **"Pre-call planning eliminated my nervousness."**

Interestingly, many people don't stop to consider what goes into planning a call. Most reps, if asked, would say that planning consists of what you are going to say to the doctor, and perhaps what data you will use to back up your points. However, one rep said that her planning consists not just of content, but of routing, appointments and access. She doesn't assume that just because Dr. Smith is normally in on Tuesdays he will be in on *this* particular Tuesday. She calls ahead to confirm. When she calls, she always tries to make an appointment, knowing that when she has an appointment the doctor is much more likely to give her some time – if for nothing else, out of a sense of obligation. She also tries to make appointments for the following month so that her schedule is pre-set. Finally, she plans her access. How is she going to get in to see this doctor? If she doesn't have an appointment and it's not an easy access office, how will she reach this physician? She has a plan. (We'll talk more about getting access in Secret #4!)

One highly successful rep who is now a Vice President in the industry said, **"Pre-call planning is essential so you can determine what areas to probe into, and remember what you talked about last so you can build your story over time. If you are organized, you can plan your next call for every physician you *might* run into the next day ... not just the ones you are targeting."** What a fantastic concept – having a targeted message for each physician you might run into at the hospital cafeteria or in the parking lot ... even if you had not planned to see them that day! Once again, *that's* the habit of a successful rep!

SUMMARY

Key Points:

- Plan your calls the night before. Include:
  - ○ Content for each call
    - ■ What will your unique message be to each doctor?
  - ○ Data sources for all content
    - ■ What material will you use to support each message?
  - ○ Routing
    - ■ Ensure each physician is scheduled to be in his or her office.
  - ○ Appointments
    - ■ Make appointments with every physician you can. Schedule future appointments so your schedule is pre-set.
  - ○ Access
    - ■ Plan *how* you will get face-to-face with each doctor.

Key Quote:

"Pre-call planning is essential so you can ... build your story over time. If you are organized, you can plan your next call for every physician you might run into ... not just the ones you are targeting."

SUCCESS ASSESSMENT

1. Presently, how well am I planning my calls?

   1   2   3   4   5   6   7   8   9   10

   Not at All   Very Thoroughly

2. Is this number where I would like it to be?

   Yes   No

3. What specific steps could I take to plan more efficiently? (Suggestions include: Set time aside each evening to plan for the next day; create a worksheet to assist in planning; stock car with all data sources I will need to back up the content of my messages, etc.)

   _____

   _____

   _____

   _____

   _____

   _____

   _____

   _____

   _____

   _____

   _____

SECRET #3:
KNOW MORE SCIENCE

Pharmaceutical companies are very careful about the information that they disseminate to their salespeople. Our industry is one of the most regulated industries in the country due to the serious nature of what we sell. If a sales representative discusses off-label information with a physician, for example, the company can face severe consequences from the FDA. Even worse, a patient could be critically harmed.

But many salespeople say they need more information than their company provides to be competitive. Is this true? If you *only* know the material that your company has given you, do you have enough to be highly successful? If not, is it appropriate to seek out more information?

The successful representatives interviewed for this book had a lot to say on this subject ... and they almost all concurred with one other – **you do need to know more information**

than your basic detail pieces provide, but you never need to detail using unapproved information.

Not one representative interviewed said that they detail off-label or even wish they could. In fact, several responded that it was completely unethical, unnecessary and could lead to serious injury to patients. However, they all believe that it is extremely important to read up on the diseases you cover, your products and the specialty you call on.

In general, the successful representatives seek out the latest information because they don't want a physician to bring up an article and get caught unaware of the data. If an article is published that shows your product in a poor light or your competitor in a better one, you need to be prepared if a physician brings it up in her office. One representative said, "I always scan the journals as soon as they come in the mail. If a physician brings up a negative issue about my product and refers to a recent article, I can say, 'Yes, I did read that article and understand your concern, but if you look here at our product circular, our Phase Three study with over 3,000 patients showed...' It lets the physician know that I am current in my field, and also lets me use that article to effectively refer back to data I *am* allowed to use."

Most representatives said that they get their information from peer-reviewed journals, CME events[3] and dinner programs. They keep up on any new information that may interest their doctors. They then use this knowledge as a

---

[3] Some companies do not allow their salespeople to attend CME events. Make sure you know your company's policy.

background to understand their physician's broader viewpoint during a detail. For example, one representative with a reputation for her scientific knowledge said, "To have an intelligent conversation it's important to know the [latest] science, but you need to be careful about what you say because **your company is liable for what you say**. Read the journals while you are in the medical school libraries, just so you know what the buzz is. You don't have to talk about the studies, or talk off-label if a physician brings one up, but you'll be in the know." Another rep concurred, saying, "Most companies do an excellent job of providing basic market knowledge, decent competitive knowledge, and in-depth product knowledge. But if you don't understand all the major issues your doctor is thinking about, and a lot of detail about your category, you will usually miss the mark."

Another representative has a solid strategy. She said, "A good rep will go beyond the parameters of what is [expected] in training. I subscribe to and read appropriate medical journals, I check our competitors' websites, and attend CME programs [to further my knowledge]." Similarly, many reps said they learn a lot of their current information by listening carefully to the physicians who speak at their dinner programs.

Finally, one representative said, "I believe that **knowledge is one of the basic building blocks in securing relationships**. It is a major component in credibility. If you can't have an intelligent discussion with a physician about your product and the therapeutic area in which you detail, then you shouldn't be there."

Managers agreed. One manager said, "The best of the best are never satisfied with what they know, how well they convey it, or how they can leverage every interaction into a commitment from the customer." Another manager said, "Reps need to be on the front of the wave. We get more kudos for having a consultative, clinical approach from physicians, but you can't do that if you don't read the journals and understand the studies."

Notice again that *none* of the reps claimed they detailed off-label or used unbalanced information to achieve their outstanding results. In fact several cautioned against it. This next story is true, sadly. An ophthalmologist prescribed a beta-blocker eye-drop to an emergent patient who couldn't speak English, and there was no interpreter to ask about her allergies or history. The beta-blocker's side effects had been played down by the representative, who reasoned, "it's only a topical beta-blocker – it's not systemic." The physician remembered this advice, figuring if the patient had an adverse reaction, it wouldn't too severe. The doctor prescribed the beta-blocker, the patient used it, had a systemic reaction, and consequently died. Now imagine, for just a moment, that you are that representative ...

The moral of the chapter is, of course, to read the current peer-reviewed journals, go to CME programs and listen to the speakers you sponsor at dinner programs. Though there is never a need to detail off-label, you need to be current to be competitive.

SUMMARY

Key Points:

- Be diligent about keeping current with the science on your product, your competitor's products and relevant disease areas.

- Keep current by:
    - Reading peer-reviewed journals as soon as they are published.
    - Attending CME programs, if your company allows.
    - Listening carefully to the speakers at your dinner programs.

- NEVER detail off-label.

Key Quote:

"Knowledge is one of the basic building blocks in securing relationships."

SUCCESS ASSESSMENT

1. How well do I know the current science relating to my products?

   1   2   3   4   5   6   7   8   9   10

   Not at All   Very Thoroughly

2. How well do I know the current science relating to my competitors' products?

   1   2   3   4   5   6   7   8   9   10

   Not at All   Very Thoroughly

3. How well do I know the current science relating to the diseases I discuss?

   1   2   3   4   5   6   7   8   9   10

   Not at All   Very Thoroughly

4. What steps can I take to be current with the data? (For example, subscribe to relevant journals, begin taking notes at dinner lectures, get a list of current CME programs at the local university, hospital, etc.)

   _____

   _____

   _____

   _____

   _____

   _____

SECRET #4:

GET IN THE DOOR

Once you have committed yourself to making solid details, you've pre-planned each call and you are current on your science, you are ready to face your doctors. But many of them are extremely difficult to see! In fact many offices, particularly in the busy primary care market, won't allow reps in at all, or will only see them over lunch. Unfortunately, there is no easy solution to this problem. However, the successful reps *did* share some excellent methods that increase their chances of getting in the door.

The one thing that sales representatives have that doctors almost always want is samples. Therefore, **the easiest way to get in the door is with your samples**. The FDA requests that pharmaceutical sales representatives witness the doctor as he signs for samples, presumably to ensure that the samples actually go to the doctor and not to an unauthorized third party. Many companies abide by this rule, so if an office won't let you see the doctor but still wants your samples, don't let them take your signature card/device back to the doctor while you wait in the lobby. Instead, tell them, "Unfortunately, my company requires that I witness the doctor as she signs for the samples." According to one rep, this works about 75% of the time. She said it is crucial that all teammates agree to follow this practice to establish continuity with the offices. Since many other companies also follow the same procedure, the offices don't balk at this request, and the rep often gains access in many otherwise fruitless situations.

If you are in a position where the doctors in a particular office don't prescribe much of your drug, make sure to leave very few samples so that they will need your samples each time you come. If the doctors don't prescribe your drug at all, and you are told, "We don't need any of your samples and the doctor is too busy to see reps right now," just ask when would be a better time ... and then *come back at exactly that time*. Announce that you have returned at the requested time, and the receptionist will usually feel obligated to let you back to see the doctor.

Another way to get in the door, particularly with doctors who don't typically see reps, is by leveraging your relationships. One smart representative said that after many years of calling on busy family practice offices, there were still some offices – *even after several years* – that had never let her in the back! She finally decided to try a new approach – leveraging relationships. She went to the doctors who she knew were friends with Dr. Hard-to-See, and asked if they had any ideas on how she could see this doctor. Sometimes the doctors would not be able to help, but on a few occasions she found that the doctors were happy to lend a hand, giving her advice on where Dr. Hard-to-See might be found outside of the clinic, and information on his personal interests. In one case, a physician even picked up the phone and called Dr. Hard-to-See on her behalf! Believe it or not, that phone call resulted in the beginning of a great relationship with that doctor.

A similar method for leveraging your relationships is to go to events that your hard-to-see doctors attend, and ask other doctors to introduce you. For example, if you are at an exhibit at a regional physician's meeting and you spot Dr. Hard-to-See, look around quickly for a doctor who might be willing to introduce you. Just *make sure that you have a plan!*

Pre-call planning (Secret #2) is particularly important for situations like the one above. If you are at your exhibit booth and Dr. Jones (your favorite doctor) walks up with Dr. Hard-to-See, make sure you know what you're going to say! You need to have a plan so that you can see Dr. Hard-to-See again. If you simply detail him and then let him walk away, he may think you are a knowledgeable person, but that won't necessarily get you in his door next week. Here is a key point about detailing hard-to-see physicians:

> **With easy-to-see physicians, your goal is to have a successful detail; with hard-to-see physicians, your goal is to have a successful detail *and* make sure you have a plan to get in the door the next time.**

Whenever you detail a hard-to-see physician, constantly ask yourself if there is something in your conversation that you can use to get back in his door in a couple of weeks. It might be further data about the disease you discussed, an article on a mutual hobby, or information about speaking for your company. Whatever it is, **make sure you find something to follow up on, and get him to commit to a time for that follow-up call**. If possible, get the doctor to commit to following up outside of his office, since his office environment is probably not rep-friendly.

Another type of office with restricted access is the type that only allows reps in the door when they are sponsoring a lunch. In these cases, the offices can be booked up to a year in advance with lunch appointments! In this situation, try using the other tactics in this chapter to see the doctors during times when you don't have an appointment, and especially try to see the doctors outside of the clinic. Furthermore, make sure to coordinate with others in your company so that if you have to cancel a lunch, others can take the timeslot instead. Additionally, invite your team members to your lunches so that if one rep gets trapped in a conversation with a receptionist, other reps are available to detail the doctors. Particularly in large offices, you will need to have several team members present so that doctors don't eat and run without hearing about your products.

Putting all of these pieces together, let's create a scenario that demonstrates how to use the tools in this chapter to get access to a hard-to-see physician. Imagine that there is a doctor who does not see reps, but is a clinical researcher and a very high prescriber of drugs in the class you sell.

First, find out who his friends are. Perhaps you can look at his diploma and find out if he went to medical school at a University where one of your friendly doctors also attended.

Second, leverage your relationships by asking one of your friends to introduce you to Dr. Hard-to-See at an upcoming meeting.

Third, plan your call. Find out as much about this doctor as you can, such as information on his research interests, patients and hobbies. Include a strategy on how you will get to see him again.

Fourth, execute your call as planned. Try saying something like, "I've been wanting to meet with you to talk about your research! I'd love to talk with you sometime about doing clinical research for our company. Do you have an interest in discussing that?" When he says, "yes" (because he probably will), plan your next meeting.

Fifth, plan your meeting somewhere away from his office. Maybe he would like to meet in the cafeteria after Grand Rounds next week.

Finally, once you have set up a time to meet, contact your manager or a research person and have them accompany you. Make sure the meeting will be fruitful for the doctor, and you will be rewarded with a reputation for providing value. Most importantly, you will probably be able to get in his door!

SUMMARY

Key Points:

- Require that you witness the doctor as he or she signs for samples. This covers you against sample fraud and will often give you an opportunity to detail the physician that you otherwise wouldn't have had.

- Leverage your relationships. Ask your favorite doctors for advice on how to see their friend, Dr. Hard-to-See. If appropriate, ask them to introduce you to him or her.

- *Always* have a plan for what you will say if you meet your hard-to-see doctors. If you unexpectedly end up in an elevator with one of them, what you say (or don't say) could be the difference between getting in the door or not.

Key Quote:

"With easy-to-see physicians, your goal is to have a successful detail; with hard-to-see physicians, your goal is to have a successful detail _and_ make sure you have a plan to get in the door the next time."

SUCCESS ASSESSMENT

Who are my 5 most difficult physicians to see?

1. _____

2. _____

3. _____

4. _____

5. _____

Name one friend or colleague of each hard-to-see physician who might give you information or help you get in to see him or her.

Hard-to-See Physician	Friend of Hard-to-See
1. _____	1. _____
2. _____	2. _____
3. _____	3. _____
4. _____	4. _____
5. _____	5. _____

On your computer, or on a separate piece of paper, write down your detail for each hard-to-see doctor and memorize it. You may run into one of them unexpectedly tomorrow! For this exercise, you may need to research a little bit more (for example, call their friends to get information).

43

SECRET #5:
TARGET YOUR MESSAGE

Imagine this scenario: You walk into the shoe department at your favorite store. A salesperson bounds up to you and excitedly and loudly tries to sell you a pair of trendy new boots while complimenting you profusely on your clothing. She has not asked you what you are looking for, and in fact, you are *not* looking for trendy boots, but for a pair of dress shoes for a black-tie affair that night. In fact, you are quite conservative, never wear anything trendy and you can't stand the boots! Furthermore, you are afraid to even try boots on because the only pair you ever owned was difficult to walk in, and you fell down some stairs in them and broke your ankle. To top it off, you are very shy, and the salesperson's boisterous personality instantly turns you off! Now ask yourself two questions:

- What is the likelihood that she will sell you something today?

- What is the likelihood that you will leave that store and shop elsewhere for your dress shoes?

Now, imagine that you are the salesperson. But instead of selling shoes, you're selling pharmaceuticals, and instead of selling in a retail store, you're selling in a doctor's office. Be honest with yourself:

Do you walk into your customers' offices with the same approach at each office, the same message to every doctor, and the same assumptions about doctors' beliefs and habits?

Differentiating your messages based on which customer you are detailing is called "targeting" your message. Imagine that targeting your message to a customer is like trying to hit a bulls-eye. If you come blazing into an office determined to sell the doctor on how efficacious your drug is, but she is more interested in the side effect profile, you'll miss the target. Or perhaps you talk about side effects, but don't discuss the one side effect that has her most concerned. In that case, you might hit the target, but not hit the bulls-eye. **You need to aim for the bulls-eye every time**.

For many reps, targeting a message may look something like this:

1. They look at the doctor's prescribing data and realize that he is writing for Product Z instead of their product.

2. They *assume* they know why the doctor likes Product Z (For example, Product Z is the most efficacious drug in the class.)

3. They construct a detail based on that assumption, and then...

4. They get in front of the doctor and present their message using the latest detail piece, talking as fast as they can, *assuming* the doctor is in a hurry and doesn't have time to have a true discussion.

5. Along the way, they may annoy doctors and/or staff by being too bouncy, aggressive or intrusive.

Successful reps describe a much different scenario. Successful representatives know the importance of targeting their messages, and understand that it can be quite an art to do it well.

When targeting a message, the first thing that successful reps do is *listen* to what the doctor is saying. In fact, **the art of listening is the most common element that successful representatives attribute to their success**. One representative said, **"Truly accurate, targeted messages require more than data from a computer. They require strategically crafted probes and keen listening skills."** Another rep commented similarly, by saying, "I think the most important thing a sales person can do is listen. Listen and watch. I try to present information but always engage a customer in conversation and then sit back and listen and watch. The tendency is to 'tell, tell, tell,' and you get nothing out of those calls. No insight into what makes your customer tick. If you engage in conversation but always listen and watch body language, you will gain a tremendous amount of insight in a much shorter time frame." Similarly, another rep said, "Some of my coworkers and other salespeople just talk, talk, talk and don't truly listen. They are waiting to speak."

So the first lesson of targeting your message is to "Ask and Listen." By asking open-ended questions, you steer your customer into a dialogue where you can listen for her true interests and concerns about your product.

Once you've learned to ask open-ended questions and listen to your doctor's responses, there are five other areas that successful reps said they take into account when targeting their messages to each individual physician:

1. Personality
2. Learning Process
3. Prescribing Continuum
4. Background Factors
5. Current Prescribing Data

Let's look at each one of these areas.

PERSONALITY

One common factor noted among successful reps regarding targeting their messages was that they try to match the doctor's personality. This is crucial because we tend to relate best to other people like ourselves. One rep said, "You have to become a different person in [each] office. You need to be quiet in some offices, very talkative in others. This is important not only to the doctors, but their staff as well."

Another rep agreed, and gives a great example of going the extra mile. She said, "I have taken a training course that has taught me that different personalities respond better to different words and phrases. I have pinpointed each doctor's [personality] and utilized these words."

One manager said that tailoring your details to each doctor's individual personality is a necessity. He said, **"If I don't [tailor my approach to each doctor], it is the equivalent of taking them to Baskin Robbins™ and ordering them all *my* favorite flavor. If I treat each customer as if they are all the same, I turn most of them off, and indicate that I'm more interested in doing things my way than theirs."**

Hopefully, this information seems obvious to you. However, there are many reps who take the same approach in every office. They are the reps who are absolutely treasured at some offices, and despised at others.

LEARNING PROCESS

The next factor that many successful reps noted regarding the topic of targeting is the importance of understanding the doctor's unique learning style. If you took a psychology course in college, you probably learned about adult learning styles. Essentially, some of us learn visually, perhaps by seeing charts and graphs. Others learn audibly, by hearing information. Some learn tactically, by doing things hands on. Some people take a big picture approach, while others like to know the minute details of what they are learning. It is important to understand each doctor's learning style if you want them to really take in your information. Some doctors love to see the colorful detail pieces with easy-to-read graphs, charts and quotes. Other doctors prefer seeing the actual detailed studies that those graphs and charts came from, so they can scour the study for the fine print. One doctor might want to have a pleasant conversation with you about your drug, while his partner might enjoy getting into a loud toe-to-toe debate with you in the hallway!

How do you determine a doctor's learning style? There are a couple of good ways. The first is to ask him indirectly. For example, when you tell a doctor that you have the latest data about your product's new indication, ask him if he prefers to see the detail piece, the actual study or if he would just like to hear about it. During the detail, you can also ask him how much information he would like to have. For example, when you mention that there were 3,342 patients in the study, ask, "Do you want to see the patient demographics?" If he is detail-oriented, he probably will.

Another, more subtle, way to get a handle on whether a doctor is an auditory or visual learner is to listen carefully to the words she chooses. For example, imagine that you are sharing data about your product. The physician might respond with something like, "I don't *see* any reason to change my mind," or "this data *looks* good." These are visual people. Auditory people might respond with something like "What I *hear* you saying is ..." or "this *sounds* like strong proof of X." Listening for these subtle verbal cues can be an easy way to uncover a doctor's learning style.

PRESCRIBING CONTINUUM

As you know, every doctor falls somewhere on a broad continuum of prescribing habits. Some doctors prescribe new drugs with confidence, while others want a 5-year, long-term safety study in their hands, perfectly designed to avoid statistical error, before they will contemplate trying it out in a few patients. For every doctor, you obviously need to understand where they are on that prescribing continuum. You will learn this information once you have been around your territory a few times, and many companies now label their customers regarding how quickly they embrace new drugs. Terms like "Early Adopter," "Tried and True" and "Driver" are examples of terms that companies use to describe doctors' prescribing habits.

But perhaps more importantly, you need to know *why* a doctor is in a particular position on the continuum. Is he hesitant to try new drugs because new drugs are typically expensive? Is she worried about a lawsuit with an unknown drug? Is his skepticism due to a relative lack of data on new drugs? Is he aggressive because he wants to be the "cowboy" in town who always does things first? Once you know *why* a doctor is in a certain position on the prescribing continuum, you are better able to target your message. You can start you details with phrases like, "I know patient safety is important to you," or "I know you'll be the first to try this new dose!" These phrases subtly tell the doctor that you understand him or her.

BACKGROUND FACTORS

Finally, there are issues every doctor has that no company or marketing department can pinpoint. These are issues that are unique to the doctor that may make him more willing or hesitant to use certain products. For example, if a doctor's mother is dying from cancer, he may be very willing to try the newest drugs for cancer, even if he is normally quite conservative. On the other hand, if a doctor had a patient die from an adverse event, he is probably much less likely to use that class of drug, even if he is normally a very aggressive prescriber. Remember that a doctor's motivation for prescribing a drug can change quickly based on things like feedback from patients, good or bad press about a drug, personal experience, advertising, another physician's input ... or a recent detail! Always assume that things are changing.

CURRENT PRESCRIBING DATA

The most obvious tool for targeting your messages is to use the most current prescribing data that your company has on your doctors. Knowing what they are prescribing, as well as the trends in their prescribing habits, is invaluable. However, it should never be the sole information you use to target your message. From the preceding pages, it should be clear that the most successful representatives use their prescribing data as one of many different tools – not their main tool – when targeting their messages.

If you have been in your territory for some time and feel like you are in a slump, a renewed vigor in targeting your messages could be just the thing you need to get the edge back in your sales game. Pay particular attention to the Success Assessment at the end of this chapter, couple your new targeting techniques with your pre-call planning, and see how much more successful your details are next week!

SUMMARY

Key Points:

- Effectively targeting your messages requires:
  - ○ Asking open-ended questions.
  - ○ *Listening* to your customer's responses.
  - ○ Using different approaches for different personalities.
  - ○ Using different approaches for different learning styles.
  - ○ Having an understanding of *where* a doctor is on the prescribing continuum and *why* he or she is there.
  - ○ Having knowledge of background factors that may affect the doctor's willingness to prescribe.
  - ○ Having knowledge of the doctor's current prescribing numbers.

Key Quote:

"If you don't tailor your approach to each doctor, it is the equivalent of taking them to Baskin Robbins™ and ordering them your favorite flavor."

SUCCESS ASSESSMENT

1. Do I talk too much, or do I listen carefully to each customer?

   1   2   3   4   5   6   7   8   9   10
   Talk Too Much   Listen

2. Do I change my personality to fit each office I work with?

   1   2   3   4   5   6   7   8   9   10
   No   Yes

3. Do I understand my doctors' learning styles?

   1   2   3   4   5   6   7   8   9   10
   No   Yes

4. Do I know *where* each doctor is on the prescribing continuum and *why* he or she is there?

   1   2   3   4   5   6   7   8   9   10
   No   Yes

5. Do I understand the background factors that affect my customers' prescribing habits?

   1   2   3   4   5   6   7   8   9   10
   No   Yes

6. Do I know the most current prescribing data for each customer?

   1   2   3   4   5   6   7   8   9   10
   No   Yes

SECRET #6:

CLOSE THE SALE

In most other industries, you simply *have* to close your call by asking for the business because that is how you prompt the customer to sign a contract or pay for a product. The pharmaceutical industry is different, however, because no contracts are signed, nor does your customer – the physician – pay for your product. The physician is simply an intermediary who controls how many people can get access to your product through prescriptions. Since he or she doesn't officially enter into a sales agreement after a detail, many reps don't close. There could be a variety of reasons for this, but the main reason is probably that...

Closing is uncomfortable.

In fact, most people would probably agree that closing is the most uncomfortable part of a sales call. Those reps who don't close often use the excuse that "doctors don't like a hard sell." But no one said that closing has to include a hard sell! And how are doctors different? *No one* likes a hard sell – not a doctor, not a janitor, not you and not me. Let's all admit that closing is simply uncomfortable. As adults, however, we should be able to overcome this fear and do what we are being paid to do! Let's hear what successful reps say about closing...

One exceptional rep is legendary in her company for nearly *doubling* the national market share average for the division's best-selling drug. She says, "*Always* [close at the end of a call] and review key messages ... tell them which patients would benefit from the product and why." Certainly her insistence on closing has contributed to her phenomenal market share.

Other reps and managers agree, saying:

- "I'm not going to walk into an office and waste my time (and theirs) by not asking for the business."

- "How can you expect to get the business if you don't ask for it?"

- "Not closing is like hitting a home run and stopping at third base. You've got to cross the plate for the run to score, and you've got to close to make the sale."

- **"If you don't ask for something, you probably won't get it."**

Clearly, the most successful reps make a serious point of closing every detail.

Several successful representatives, however, point out that you must earn the right to close. "I only close at the end of the call if I have earned the right to close. I must feel that I have actually overcome the doctor's objections and given him a good reason to prescribe my product before I will ask for the business."

Another rep, who won 2nd place in *Pharmaceutical Representative* Magazine's "Pharmaceutical Representative of the Year" contest, has a similar point of view. He says, **"Closing is an earned privilege. When I have given sufficient reason to request a specific action, it is completely valid. To not ask for action is to waste both my customer's and my time, and greatly waste my company's resources. If I am afraid to close, I must ask myself if I truly belong in sales..."**

If you refer back to Chapter 1, on making details instead of calls, you should recognize that every time you successfully detail a physician, you should also close. In fact, don't count it as a successful detail unless you close! However, if you don't have time for a detail, it would be silly to ask for the business.

So how, exactly, should you close? Make sure that your close conforms to the following guideline:

After you have successfully detailed the doctor and given her a reason to use the drug, ask for the business...

1. Directly, and
2. In a way that makes you both feel comfortable.

It is essential that you directly ask for the business. Something like, "Have I shown you today that Product X is a great choice for elderly patients with high blood pressure?" does not go far enough. You must ask *directly* for the business. To that last sentence add, "Great! Then will you please prescribe Product X for those elderly patients we discussed today?"

Everyone has different phrasing that makes them – and their doctors – feel comfortable. Here are a few examples of closing lines that you can use from some of the most successful reps in the country:

> "Thank you for your time today. Can I count on your business for patients with high blood pressure that are contraindicated to a beta-blocker?"

> "I'm glad you agree that the side effect profile of Product X is the best in the oral contraceptive class. Can I please ask you to prescribe Product X in those patients where side effects are of particular concern to you?"

> "Dr. Smith, now that we have agreed on the benefits of Drug X for your GERD patients, I'm excited to tell you that it is now covered under [XYZ formulary plan]. Will you please make sure to prescribe Drug X for patients on that plan?"

You get the idea. Close in a way that is comfortable for both you and the doctor, but just make sure that you are direct!

SUMMARY

Key Points:

- At the end of the day, don't count a detail in your computer unless you closed at the end of it.

- After you have successfully detailed the doctor and given her a reason to use the drug, ask for the business directly and in a way that makes you feel comfortable.

Key Quote:

"If you don't ask for something, you probably won't get it!"

SUCCESS ASSESSMENT

Do I currently close at the end of every detail?

Never   Sometimes   Often   Usually

What are three closing lines that I feel comfortable using with different personality types?

1. _____

_____

_____

_____

2. _____

_____

_____

_____

3. _____

_____

_____

_____

SECRET #7:

DON'T GET TOO CLOSE!

No, this chapter is not about personal space. It's about relationships. Most people say that being successful in sales is all about building relationships. But successful salespeople don't agree. They say that relationships are only part of the equation. Of course, quality relationships are crucial to building rapport and respect, but successful reps (and their managers) have found that developing close friendships can often actually be detrimental. Consider this story from a twenty-year veteran …

"I became good friends with a doctor when I first started. We played golf, went to lunch, etc. Every time I was in his clinic, we chatted about everything but product. When he retired, I saw him and asked him why he never prescribed my products much, since we were good friends. He answered, 'You never really asked me to prescribe your drugs!' I learned a lesson from that."

That story beautifully illustrates the inherent problem with building close friendships with your customers. Once the relationship becomes more personal than professional, it can become very uncomfortable to discuss product and especially to ask for the business. Even people who are not shy about closing can find it hard to close their own friends. It just feels like you are using their friendship for your professional gain. Therefore, most reps don't detail their good friends and assume that their "friends" will support them by prescribing their product.

One representative, while discussing this problem said, "I always try to develop a personal relationship with my customers, but I make sure that it is never more than 49% of the relationship. If I can get each relationship to be 49% personal and 51% professional, then I am in a perfect situation to enjoy the relationship, yet still capitalize on it by asking for the business."

There are, of course, a small handful of reps who can build those strong personal relationships, yet still look the doctor in the eye and say, "I need to change the topic to business...," and then ask directly for the business. If that sounds like you, keep it up. But if you tend, like most people, to find it difficult to ask your friends for their business, it's better to keep your relationships at least 51% professional.

One manager emphasizes this point. He says, "If [a relationship] becomes too close, we might lose some objectivity. Then reps might leave the sales data on the table, and feel they can *expect* the business and don't need to *earn* it anymore. **Don't ever assume that when a relationship develops into a personal relationship that you can quit selling. Never assume the business is yours forever.**"

So what do you do if you have already formed some of those close friendships where you are too uncomfortable to ask for the business? One idea is to make a 3-call effort to turn it around. In the first call, instead of just talking about family and fun, also tell them that you are excited about things that are going on with work – for example, your product is doing well and your company has new information coming out soon. In the second call, tell them that you brought the new information you previously told them about, and detail them. In the third call, detail them again with different information, and close at the end. You can still discuss personal topics while you are with them, but adding in these elements over the course of three calls should comfortably get you back into the position of detailing them.

Another idea is to ask them for their professional advice. Tell them that you have been given new information on your product, and would like them to review it and give you their honest opinion about what it means, whether it's credible, etc. This will force them to read something carefully about your product and *think* about it.

Perhaps the best approach is to be more direct and honest. Simply say, "You know, you've become such a good friend that I forget to tell you about my products..." or "You've become such a good friend that I get embarrassed to detail you on my products, but I still need to do that because it's my job!" A third way to word it might be, "Since you've become such a good friend, I feel embarrassed to detail you on my products, but I know that I've got some really good information that you can use when making decisions for your patients. If it's okay with you, I'm going to make sure that when we're in your office I begin telling you about my products again, but when we're outside of your office, I'll only discuss work if you bring up the topic." Put yourself in the physician's shoes. If you were the physician, you would probably completely understand, and actually have a lot of respect for the person!

In conclusion, it's important to realize that your job is to detail the physicians who are your friends with the same energy and regularity as you detail those physicians whom you only know professionally. If you have found yourself in a position with some of your doctors where they have become such good friends that you don't feel comfortable detailing them anymore, use one of the approaches outlined above to re-establish the professional portion of your relationship. If you are a newer rep who has not yet established close relationships with your customers, or are a more experienced rep who is moving to a new territory, keep in mind that you should never let the relationship progress to a point where you are too embarrassed to ask for the business!

SUMMARY

Key Points:

- Personal relationships with your customers can help you earn their rapport and respect.

- Always try to keep relationships with your customers no more than 49% personal and no less than 51% professional. This will allow you to prosper from the benefits of friendship, while still feeling comfortable enough to ask for the business.

- If you are currently in a position where you are not detailing certain physicians because they are close friends, use one of the following tactics to get back on track:
    - Use the three-call approach to slowly begin talking product with them again.
    - Ask for their professional advice about your products on a regular basis.
    - Be direct. Tell them that you need to begin detailing them again, even though they are a good friend – it's your job!

Key Quote:

"Don't ever assume that when a relationship develops into a personal relationship that you can quit selling. Never assume the business is yours forever."

SUCCESS ASSESSMENT

1. List the physicians whom you know on a personal level (For example, physicians who invite you to their home, have introduced you to their family and call you with some frequency.) Then answer whether you still ask for their business:

PHYSICIAN NAME   DO I STILL ASK FOR HIS
                                  OR HER BUSINESS?

_____   Yes   No

_____   Yes   No

_____   Yes   No

_____   Yes   No

_____   Yes   No

_____   Yes   No

_____   Yes   No

2. What approach will I use to get personal relationships back to a place where I feel comfortable detailing?

_____

_____

_____

_____

_____

SECRET #8:
BE POSITIVE

One thing you can guarantee about the pharmaceutical industry is that it will always be changing. New formulary decisions, new FDA policies, new political agendas, new competitors, new drug classes, new side effects, new territories, new team mates...

Change can be traumatic, but to enjoy your job and be successful, you *must* deal with change effectively – and it is essential that you maintain a positive attitude. This is perhaps the one area that most distinctly separates exceptional reps from average reps.

When asked about her 20 years of experience in the industry, the vice president of a major pharmaceutical company noted that top performers have a very positive and optimistic outlook. When business issues arise, they always look at the positive aspect of the situation versus focusing on the negative. The glass is always half full for them.

Additionally, she noted that the best representatives "approach their business with both short- and long-term perspectives in mind. They manage to meet their short-term goals in order to make their [quotas] each year, but they always spend time sowing the seeds for the long-term and future business opportunities. They do a terrific job looking for new business opportunities while staying focused and disciplined on the fundamentals. They know that high performance is a combination of calling on the right customers, with the right message at the right frequency." On the other side of the coin, negative representatives rarely look at the long term because they are too focused on all of the horrible things happening to them in the present!

If you would like to be identified as one of your company's superstars, then you absolutely must become known as a positive person. Your attitude will be most telling when challenges arise. As the saying goes, **"You can tell a man's character in times of hardship."** If your company has to pull a drug off the market, your sales quota is increased half way through the year or you've been told you can no longer take doctors out to dinner, your manager will take note of the people who *don't* complain, simply because so few won't. Set yourself apart. You don't have to be a Pollyanna, telling everyone to see the bright side of the rainbow, but let your manager know that you understand the reasons behind the change, and that you will work to find new ways to grow the business given the new constraints. Your manager will not only be incredibly grateful, but will probably talk about you to his or her peers, setting you up for a promotion or an award.

One manager tells of a representative he managed who had been vying for the company's top award (Vice President's Club) for many years. He worked very hard in his territory, but for years his sales and market share numbers never quite made it to the top. After about five years, his perseverance finally paid off, and his numbers met the criteria to be considered for the award. However, numbers were not the only factor in achieving the award at his company. A full 30% was subjective, including taking on extra projects, mentoring new reps and exhibiting leadership qualities. The big wild card in receiving the award was that each person voted into the Vice President's Club had to be approved by the entire management team. While this representative had the numbers, the projects and the mentoring under his belt, his bad attitude was what he was known for around the company. The management team voted almost unanimously *not* to admit him into the club. If you've been in the industry for a few years, you can probably name at least one person who is like the gentleman in the story above. Don't let a bad attitude keep you from the recognition you otherwise deserve.

Sometimes, however, we are blind to our own faults. How do you know if you are branded for having a negative attitude? One way is to look critically at your actions. Are you the first to raise your hand and complain? Are you always playing the role of "devil's advocate" at your meetings? Has anyone ever made a snide comment about your attitude or your need to express your opinions? Do you regularly roll your eyes or scowl during meetings? Are you sarcastic and cynical? If you answered "yes" to any of these questions, you are likely known for having a bad attitude, or at least not acknowledged for having a positive one!

Still unsure? Ask one or two trusted colleagues to be candid with you. Make sure that the people you ask work closely enough with you to witness your attitude in action.

Remember, however, that you don't just want to avoid being known for having a bad attitude – you want to be recognized for having a positive attitude! Being in the middle of the attitude continuum is not where you want to be. If you suspect you are anywhere but at the "Highly Positive" end, here are some tips to change your attitude ... and people's perceptions of it:

1. Be Vocal. Let people know that you plan to change. Tell them, "You know, we're going through a really challenging time right now with our product launch being postponed again, and I've decided that from now on, I'm going to keep a positive attitude about it. **If there's nothing I can do to solve the problem right now, I am not going to dwell on it!**" If you don't announce to everyone that you are planning a major attitude overhaul, it could literally take years for people to notice. Once you announce it, they may be skeptical that you will actually change, but after a few months of seeing your new attitude in action, they will become believers.

2. Get Support. Hopefully you have supportive family members, friends, colleagues and loved ones. If you can rely on a small handful of them to help you reach your goals, they can take you far. Tell each person in this trusted group that you are seriously trying to change your attitude and become more positive. Ask them to be forthright and honest when

they hear negativity creeping into your conversations. Vow to be open to their criticism and do not get defensive. An attitude is simply a habit. It can be a hard habit to change, but it can definitely be done. Use your support group to help you.

3. <u>Quit Lying with Dogs</u>. There's a saying, **"If you lie down with dogs, you'll get up with fleas."** Do not hang out with people at company functions (or in any area of your life) who are cynical, sarcastic and negative. Befriend the top reps in your company and spend your time with them.

4. <u>Utilize motivational materials</u>. This topic was already discussed in Chapter 1, but it's worth repeating. Read and listen to motivational books about how to create a positive attitude. Find some authors that speak to your style and read everything they ever wrote. Try authors like Keith Harrell, Zig Ziglar and Anthony Robbins. Their advice can revolutionize your life! A great quote from Anthony Robbins is, **"Wherever you focus, that's where you'll go."** Focus on the positive.

Given all the advice above, the single best way to change your attitude is with persistence. You will find that, as with any habit, negativity will continually try to haunt you. However, you *do* have the power to overcome it! Anthony Robbins suggests a 10-day challenge. Vow to be positive for 10 days in a row. Every time you catch yourself dwelling on a negative thought, start the 10 days over again. See how long it takes you to make it through 10 days!

SUMMARY

Key Points:

- A positive attitude is perhaps the single biggest factor that separates exceptional reps from average reps.

- In times of change, be vigilant about keeping your attitude in check. It is in these difficult times that you have the ability to stand out from the rest of the pack.

- If you have a negative attitude, try the following techniques to change your attitude, as well as people's perceptions of it:
  - Be vocal about your intent to change.
  - Get support from trusted friends and family. Have them tell you when your negative attitude is creeping back in.
  - Quit "Lying with Dogs." At company functions, spend your time with the top performers.
  - Utilize motivational materials.
  - Be persistent! Take the 10-day attitude challenge!

Key Quote:

"Wherever you focus, that's where you'll go."
– Anthony Robbins

SUCCESS ASSESSMENT

1. Answer the following questions:

Are you always the first to complain?	Yes No
Do you always play "devil's advocate"?	Yes No
Do people joke about your attitude?	Yes No
Are you cynical and sarcastic at work?	Yes No

2. If you answered "yes" to any of the above questions, you probably need to work on your attitude. Rate yourself on the following continuum. Then ask a trusted friend to rate you.

Highly Negative	Neutral	Highly Positive

   |———————|———————|———————|———————|

3. List people you can rely on for trusted advice about and support with your attitude.

   _____

   _____

   _____

4. Research and list motivational books or tapes that you plan to use:

   _____

   _____

   _____

Secret #9:
Be Ethical

One of the basic rules of successful pharmaceutical salespeople, *particularly* in today's strict environment, is to never compromise on ethics.

Most people believe that they are ethical, but there is a wide range in people's definition of "ethics." One person might *never* use a company-bought stamp for a personal letter, while another feels justified "padding" their expense account for various personal expenses. In this industry, there are many areas where ethics can be called into question, and some of them – like your samples, for instance – can cost you your job. Misusing samples or intentionally misreporting them is a crime!

One common way that some reps have been known to be unethical is detailing outside of their products' labeling. This practice can not only get you fired, but doctors will also know what you are up to and will subsequently lose respect for you.

Another common mistake, similar to detailing off-label, is detailing from scientifically questionable literature. Companies don't usually distribute poorly designed studies for their reps to detail from (although it can happen), yet reps will find studies in the journals that make a point they would like to convey, and detail from those studies.

There are three major problems with detailing off-label and using questionable literature:

1. Unless the information has been approved by DDMAC (Division of Drug Marketing, Advertising and Communications), you are not allowed to detail from it.

2. Most doctors will recognize the scientific weakness of the information, and subsequently not trust you. If they don't recognize the weakness of the information, your competitors will make sure they do.

3. Detailing using poor studies sheds a bad light on the industry. We all know doctors who won't see *any* reps because they think reps are all untrustworthy. Make sure you are not contributing to that bad perception!

This advice goes not only for you as a rep, but also for your speakers. Do *not* let your speakers discuss weak studies. Since educational dinner programs are one of the best ways to reach your customers, be sure you sponsor extremely high quality programs.

On the topic of speakers, the FDA also regulates speaker programs. For your consideration, below is a list of examples of false or misleading practices from the FDA. While this list is rather long, it's worth reading. Keep in mind that it was created for the purpose of guiding physicians who speak for pharmaceutical companies, but it should guide your details as well:

1. Representing or suggesting that a drug is safer or more effective than has been demonstrated in its package circular, whether or not such representation is made by comparison with other drugs.

2. Making specific drug comparisons of safety or efficacy without two or more adequate and well-controlled studies.

3. Containing outdated opinions about a drug or references that are more favorable to the drug than has been demonstrated in its package circular.

4. Selectively presenting information in order to make a drug appear to be safer than has been demonstrated in its package circular.

5. Misrepresenting the significance of a study by making the study appear to represent more general experience with a drug than it actually does.

6. Misrepresenting the effectiveness of the drug by failing to disclose available information that the results of a study may be due to concomitant therapy or a placebo effect.

7. Presenting data from non-clinical studies in a manner suggesting that such data has clinical significance when, in fact, no such significance has been demonstrated.

8. Not updating authoritative opinions concerning a drug by noting more recent but less favorable opinions by the same authority.

9. Using quotes or paraphrases out of context so as to mislead.

10. Using an irrelevant study to attempt to support a claim.

11. Recommending an unapproved use of a drug.

12. Broadening the indications for a combination drug by discussing the indications for the individual ingredients rather than limiting the claims to those approved for the fixed combination.

13. Using studies on normal subjects without disclosing that the subjects were normal.

14. Pooling data and statistics from dissimilar studies in order to imply larger studies than were actually conducted.

15. Using statistics erroneously to claim clinical equivalence or denying the existence of actual clinical differences.

16. Comparing two drugs on the basis of differences that have no established clinical significance.

17. Using data gained in studies where patients were treated with other than recommended dosages.

18. Using graphic matter in slides in a way that is misleading.

19. Recommending a dosage approved for use in one type of patient in another type of patient for whom it is not approved.

20. Using general terms to describe specific contra-indications and side effects.

21. Using an inadequate study to support a favorable conclusion.

22. Using a claim of "statistical significance" when there is no clinical significance.

23. Using statistical evaluations from studies, particularly retrospective ones, that are inadequate for such analysis.

24. Presenting misleading impressions from tables or graphs in slides.

25. Presenting inappropriate or invalid use of statistics.

26. Using unestablished claims regarding mechanism of action or site of drug action without disclosing that such claims are unestablished.

27. Providing insufficient emphasis on balance or disclosure due to over-emphasis of efficacy or safety.

28. Misleading use of published or unpublished reports as authentic or authoritative.

Obviously, the FDA takes speaker content very seriously! The content of your speakers' talks is the responsibility of your company. Whoever is assigned to cover speaker content is responsible for what that speaker says behind the lectern. There is nothing worse than going through the extensive planning of having a dinner program only to have your customers later chastise you for the quality of the speaker. Make sure your programs, like your daily work, are of high standards and ethics.

Beyond the content of your programs and details, there are many other areas where ethics are called into question in a pharmaceutical job. Expenses, hours worked and the number of physicians you report on your call sheet are just a few. **In general, it is best to assume that there are no grey areas. If you question whether something is ethical or allowed, either ask for your manager's approval or don't do it.** Do *not* ask your colleagues for advice (especially if you are new to the industry) because you might not know if you are asking an ethical colleague and whether you are getting sound advice!

Pharmaceutical jobs are highly coveted and very hard to get. Do not lose your job due to a shady expense report or off-label detailing. If you are ever tempted to do something unethical, even if it seems small, ask yourself, **"Is the value I will gain from this action worth more to me than my reputation?"** If the answer is "No," and it always should be, then don't do it. A wise person once said, **"Never sell your reputation because you'll never be able to afford to buy it back."**

SUMMARY

Key Points:

- In pharmaceutical sales, assume that everything is black and white, and there are no grey areas.

- Never detail using off-label information or unapproved literature.

- Don't sell your good reputation by cheating on your expense reports, misrepresenting the number of physicians you detailed or committing some other unethical act. It's simply not worth it.

- If you question whether something is ethical or allowed, either ask for your manager's approval or don't do it.

Key Quote:

"Never sell your reputation – you will never be able to afford to buy it back."

SUCCESS ASSESSMENT

Ask yourself the following questions:

1. Do I ever cheat on my expense report, even over a few stamps?

2. Do I ever misrepresent the true number of physicians I saw or details I made on a given day?

3. Do I ever misuse or misreport my samples in any way?

4. Do I ever use unapproved literature when detailing?

5. Do I ever encourage my speakers to discuss things that I am not allowed to discuss myself?

If you answered "Yes" to any of the questions above, vow at this time to change your ways immediately. Anything you gain from being unethical is simply not worth losing your reputation ... or your job.

Secret #10:
Enjoy Your Job

Many people believe that **the best way to be truly successful in your career is to enjoy what you do**. It seems logical to assume that if you *really* enjoy your sales job, you probably love the entire sales process, including prospecting, identifying a need, overcoming objections and closing. Additionally, you will enjoy getting an edge over the competition by pre-planning your calls, targeting your messages and learning additional science. People who enjoy their jobs get a tremendous rush from hearing about a patient success story, concluding a great call, and seeing their numbers improve.

A career in pharmaceutical sales is exciting and challenging. Few jobs hold the thrill of launching a new medication, or the challenge of combating a new competitor to your best-selling drug. The industry is always advancing, and you know that the products you sell result in a better quality of life and less mortality among patients. As a rep, you get to work in an intellectually stimulating field with very bright and interesting people. You have the autonomy to work from your home, see different people every day and get out in the fresh air. You'll never have to worry about being confined to a cubical all day, and if there is a colleague you don't care for, you won't have to see him or her very often!

None of the successful reps interviewed actually said "I enjoy my job, and that is why I am successful." However, when asked, "What do you see less successful reps do that you believe hinder their success?" many responded with phrases like:

- "They let themselves become apathetic"
- "They look for shortcuts and are lazy"
- "They are not excited about their products"
- "They work a 4-T hour work week instead of a 40-hour work week." (The four T's are Tuesday and Thursday from Ten until Two.)

These phrases don't describe people who are simply missing the mark when targeting their details, or pre-planning their calls, for example. They describe the actions of people who don't enjoy what they are doing enough to put in the effort that is needed to be successful.

When asked what he thinks less successful reps do to hinder their success, one manager said, "They atrophy ... They don't want to change or do anything differently. They allow themselves to fall into a rut. A rut is just a grave with longer ends."

Similarly, one vice president said that average reps "have an undue focus on looking for the 'magic bullet.' They spend too much time thinking that there will be one major formulary win, customer victory or upside in their territory that will make them successful. Simply put, they are not willing to put the time into a consistent and sustained effort in their job."

Do you recognize yourself in any of the descriptions above? Hopefully not, but if you do, it's time for a change. If you suspect that you are in a slump, it's time to pick yourself up and move forward! Many salespeople before you have picked themselves up (sometimes from the very bottom of the pack) and marched straight to the top of their sales force. You can do it too! The best place to start is by taking the "Success Assessments" at the end of each chapter in this book, and filling them out thoughtfully. In fact, it might be best to work on one Success Assessment each week. This strategy will give you time to truly implement the changes suggested in each chapter. **To reinvigorate your attitude and your performance, you need a plan, and that is *exactly* what this book is here to help you create!**

For those of you reading this book who do enjoy your job, you are in an outstanding position to propel yourself to the top ... or to stay there! There is an excellent chance that your passion for your job translates into effort in your territory. More than anything else, your passion and excitement about your products and your career will make you successful!

SUMMARY

Key Points:

- Pharmaceutical sales jobs are exciting and challenging. The industry is always advancing and you can feel good knowing that your products help improve the quality of life and decrease mortality among patients. Additionally, a pharmaceutical sales job allows you to:
  - ○ Work in an intellectually stimulating environment, with bright and interesting people.
  - ○ Work from home.
  - ○ Meet with different people each day.
  - ○ Get out in the fresh air.

- If needed, create a plan to renew your enthusiasm. Go back over the Success Assessments from each of the previous chapters, completing one each week.

- Facts tell, but passion sells! Share your passion for your products with your customers.

Key Quote:

"The best way to be truly successful in your career is to enjoy what you do."

SUCCESS ASSESSMENT

Go back over the Success Assessment at the end of each of the previous chapters. Complete one Success Assessment each week for the next nine weeks. Stay focused on making the appropriate changes for each chapter. This exercise will renew your enthusiasm, establish the habits you need for long-term success, and help you to reach your goals!

Conclusion

After months of tracking down the country's top reps, interviewing them and recording their answers, I sat back and read all the interviews at one time. I was devastated. I thought to myself, "Secrets of Successful Pharmaceutical Salespeople? *There are no secrets here!* These reps are just doing exactly what their companies are telling them to do!" For a couple of days I pondered what to do.

Then it hit me. This *IS* the secret! These superstar reps *are doing exactly what their companies tell them to do, every day!* These reps don't let themselves become lazy or apathetic with time. Every day, the most successful sales representatives:

- Strive to make every clinic visit a detail instead of a call.
- Target their messages.
- Pre-plan their calls.
- Stay current with the science.
- Work hard and creatively to get access into the clinics.
- Close at the end of every call.
- Keep their relationships professional.
- Never compromise their ethics.
- Maintain a positive attitude.
- Enjoy their job.

In short, the best reps in the country do exactly what their companies are telling them to do, every day, without exception, without excuses and without failure.

So I challenge you to emulate their results. You know their secrets. In fact, you've known them all along. The real secret is to simply put them to use!

Happy Selling!

Sarah Taylor

TAYLOR PRESENTATIONS
QUICK ORDER FORM

Secrets of Successful Pharmaceutical Salespeople

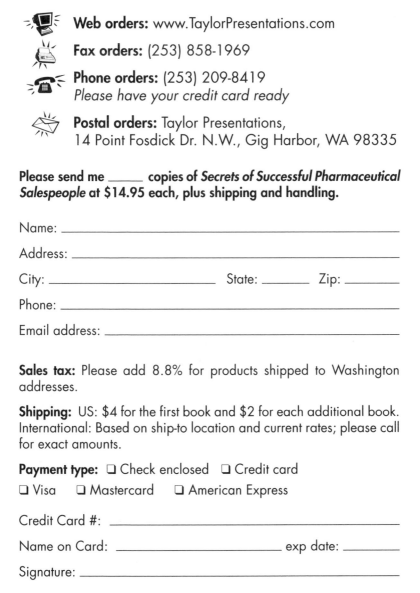

Web orders: www.TaylorPresentations.com

Fax orders: (253) 858-1969

Phone orders: (253) 209-8419
Please have your credit card ready

Postal orders: Taylor Presentations,
14 Point Fosdick Dr. N.W., Gig Harbor, WA 98335

Please send me _____ **copies of *Secrets of Successful Pharmaceutical Salespeople* at $14.95 each, plus shipping and handling.**

Name: _____

Address: _____

City: _____ State: _____ Zip: _____

Phone: _____

Email address: _____

Sales tax: Please add 8.8% for products shipped to Washington addresses.

Shipping: US: $4 for the first book and $2 for each additional book. International: Based on ship-to location and current rates; please call for exact amounts.

Payment type: ❑ Check enclosed ❑ Credit card
❑ Visa   ❑ Mastercard   ❑ American Express

Credit Card #: _____

Name on Card: _____ exp date: _____

Signature: _____

Please send more information on: ❑ Speaking ❑ Training ❑ Consulting

ABOUT SARAH TAYLOR

Sarah Taylor is a professional speaker and trainer, and the owner of Taylor Presentations, a company specializing in pharmaceutical sales motivation. She has previous experience in sales, sales management and training from a variety of industries. From 1995 to 2004, Sarah worked for Merck & Co., Inc., first in primary care sales, then in specialty sales, and finally as a Health Science Associate. She left Merck in 2004 to start Taylor Presentations.

Sarah has a Master's degree in Business Administration from Seattle University and an undergraduate business degree from the University of Washington. Her master's thesis was published in the *Journal of Ocular Pharmacology and Therapeutics*[4].

On a personal note, Sarah enjoys vegan cooking, scuba diving and adventure travel. She has been married since 2000, and lives in Gig Harbor, Washington with her husband and many pets.

Sarah can present *The Secrets of Successful Pharmaceutical Salespeople* as a keynote speech at your next sales meeting or as a customized training program for advanced or new-hire representatives. You can contact Sarah for further information at Sarah@TaylorPresentations.com or 253-209-8419.

---

[4] Taylor SA, Galbraith SM, Mills RP. Causes of non-compliance with drug regimens in glaucoma patients: a qualitative study. J Ocul Pharmacol Ther. 2002 Oct;18(5):401-9.

WHAT OTHERS ARE SAYING
ABOUT SARAH TAYLOR

"Sarah's infectious positive attitude coupled with her superior communication skills and knowledge of the pharmaceutical industry render her a highly valuable asset to any company's training and motivational needs."

Richard W. Bowne
Executive Business Manager (Retired)
Merck & Co. Inc.

"Sarah motivates by speaking to your sense of reasoning. She feeds your heart and spirit. Growth-oriented people are always anxious to hear what she will share next."

Terri Dunevant
Toastmasters International Area Governor

"Sarah Taylor brings intelligence, initiative and industry to the table. But most of all, she brings attitude – the right attitude. This wonderful attitude ... brings the best out of all those that work with her."

Alfredo Sadun, MD, PhD
Professor of Ophthalmology and Neurological Surgery
University of Southern California

"Sarah Taylor's in-depth knowledge of the pharmaceutical industry, combined with the perfect blend of professionalism and positive attitude, results in the right formula for success."

George A. Cioffi, MD
Chief of Ophthalmology
Devers Eye Institute

If you are considering hiring
Sarah Taylor to speak or train at
your company, you can read more
about what others are saying at

www.TaylorPresentations.com